CH00870636

Light in the
Darkness?

Rin Donelan

14· Oct 2016

Light
in the
Darkness?

Bill Donaldson

MAKAR PUBLISHING
Edinburgh

For Sarah

First published in Great Britain, 2005
by Makar Publishing
12 Corstorphine High Street
Edinburgh, EH12 7ST

BRITISH LIBRARY CATALOGUING IN PUBLICATION DATA
A catalogue record for this book is available from the British Library

Cover images by kind permission of the artist, John Lowrie
Morrison. *Sunset – Sound of Jura from Carsaig* and *Fladda
Lighthouse* © John Lowrie Morrison

Set in Utopia with Gorey display
Design and pre-press production by
Makar Publishing Production

Printed and bound in Great Britain by Cromwell Press

Contents

Foreword by the Very Rev. John D. Miller   *ix*
Introduction   *xi*
Acknowledgements   *xiii*

Justice and Peace
Anonymous   *2*
Arms sales   *3*
Beslan   *4*
A bombshell   *5*
Crusading   *6*
Judgement   *7*
A new rallying call   *8*
The prize   *9*
Race   *10*
1789   *11*
The Question   *12*
When?   *13*

Make Poverty History
Geldof   *15*
Corruption   *16*
Enough   *17*
Evangelical   *18*
Gordon Brown   *19*
Face to face   *20*
Greed   *21*
The hairs of our head   *22*
Heaven   *23*

Hypocrisy   *24*
3 a.m. again   *25*
Trade Justice   *26*
The Wall   *27*

A Time to Smile
Bladon Races   *29*
Golf: The Bishop of London   *30*
Chocolate biscuits   *31*
Jazz   *32*
London Town   *33*
Sir Malcolm Rifkind   *34*
Misalliance   *35*
Pocket money   *36*
Pillion ride   *37*
No smoke without fire   *38*
The Old Firm   *39*
71   *40*
Tantrums   *41*
A time to smile   *42*
Up in the morning early   *43*

A Time to Think
Aims   *45*
The butterfly   *46*
Creation   *47*
Enemies   *48*
Free–falling   *49*
Enlightenment   *50*
Labels   *52*
Mixed blessings   *53*
Message to the USA   *54*

Scots wha hae   *55*
Water   *56*

A Time to Listen
Guantanamo Bay   *58*
The present   *60*
A time to listen   *61*
The secret garden   *62*
Spin   *63*
London   *64*

Buds of Heaven
Anno Domini   *66*
Be still   *68*
Beauty   *69*
Christmas – or God with us   *70*
A gift   *71*
Homecoming   *72*
God's rainbow   *73*
Inside out   *74*
The mountain top   *75*
Renewables   *76*
Resurrection   *77*
Candles   *78*
Pope John Paul the Second   *79*

Cycling Singalong
Jubilee Scotland   *80*
Cycling Along   *81*

Foreword

This excellent book is the creation of an extraordinary man. In his Booker Prize-winning novel *The Remains of the Day* Kazuo Ishiguro writes, 'Ask any working man what is the best part of the day, and he'll tell you: "The evening, when the work is all done".' Not for Bill Donaldson a quiet retirement after his long career in education, resting now at ease with his work all done. No. At this retired stage of his life he has found himself driven to write poetry. For him a new work has begun.

This second volume of poems continues many of the themes which asserted themselves in his first book, *Does Life Make Sense?* Global trade and its causal links with global poverty, the difficulty of squaring faith in a loving God with the continuing catastrophes of international politics. And throughout this latest volume a mature Christian faith reflects on the consumerism of our secular culture, and considers the questions raised on the frontiers of scientific research.

In the poem entitled 'Heaven' a line distils one of his major concerns. Bill Donaldson is aware that Western consumer culture, heedless of the environmental cost of expanding material production, bears within it the seeds of its own destruction: *'Conspicuous consumption will one day end this heaven on earth.'* He is a moralist of the most effective kind: he directs people to see how responsible behaviour is instrumental to their own wellbeing.

In other poems Bill Donaldson draws out universal themes from contemporary news, and he can suddenly surprise and shock you. Reflecting on the terror associated with Al Qaeda he questions some of our quick assumptions. In an adaptation of one of the best-known lines of Robert

Burns, he asks, '*O' wad some power the Giftie gie us, to see oursels as Bin Laden sees us.*'

Some of these poems are carefully worked, others seem to have been dashed off in immediate reaction to a news item. But a remarkable and rare quality is common to them all. Many commentators have charted the evaporation of Christian influence from Western culture. In these poems we are presented with an outlook consistently Christian. Without apology, and with the assurance of long experience, Bill Donaldson's observations on the contemporary world are offered from a perspective of faith: he is comfortable expressing the image of Jesus Christ the teacher and the Son of God. And on the foundation of his Christian faith Bill Donaldson builds an attitude of hope despite the dark age he charts, and its dark events.

He is not content, however, merely to offer the thinking that lies within these poems. He wants a practical outcome as well. From the sale of each copy of his poems the sum of £2.00 will be donated to Christian Aid. I hope that many people will buy this book. They will help the causes and campaigns of Christian Aid, but they will also find material here to stimulate their minds and stir their souls.

Very Rev. John D. Miller
Former Moderator of the Church of Scotland

Introduction

*'Like slavery and apartheid, poverty is not natural. It is man-made
and it can be overcome and eradicated by actions of human beings.'*
Nelson Mandela, Trafalgar Square, February 2005.

When 30,000 children are dying each day from preventable
poverty, something has to be done. On July 2 in Edinburgh
something *was* done. There was a massive, united gathering in
support of a peaceful campaign against global poverty. Few
can have anticipated that more than 200,000 people would
form a continuous circle of white around the centre of the city.
Even the doubters were touched by that day and the hope it
brought. At the end of the day there was a clear message to the
G-8 at Gleneagles.

After the light the darkness. On the Monday and Tuesday a
few hundred anarchists with their black hoods, black shirts
and black hearts caused damage in both Edinburgh and
Stirling. They diverted attention from the real issues and their
behaviour was condemned by the leaders of the official
campaign.

Make Poverty History, the U.K. coalition of the world-wide
Global call to Action against Poverty, is the latest in a series of
mass movements dating back to the nineteenth century. William
Wilberforce and his Christian campaigners, the Clap- ham Sect,
fought for thirty years to achieve the Abolition of Slavery. In 1833,
Wilberforce himself was on his deathbed when the Bill was
introduced by Thomas Buxton to abolish slavery throughout the
British territories.

There is an interesting link between slavery abolition and
the Jubilee 2000 campaign to abolish debt in the developing

world. Martin Dent, who founded Jubilee 2000 in 1992 was the great-great-great grandson of Thomas Buxton. Martin and his co-founder, Bill Peters, saw the debt crisis in the developing world as the new slavery. Both are men of faith and ability but even they cannot have anticipated where such tiny beginnings would lead. Within a decade the Jubilee campaign spread across the world with 140 countries involved and a record 24 million signatures on the Jubilee Debt Petition

Now in the twenty-first century there is a new momentum and a broader vision building on these earlier campaigns. The Millennium Development Goals are the foundation stones of the current campaign to achieve Trade Justice, further Debt Cancellation and more and better Aid. The end of apartheid in South Africa and the destruction of the Berlin Wall have inspired a new generation to realise that popular movements can influence the decisions of world leaders. Gleneagles may yet prove to be a significant step in the battle to secure justice for the poorest on earth.

The book of verse I published in 2003, *Does Life Make Sense?*, raised over £2,000 for Christian Aid. I am grateful to all who supported that venture so generously.

This new book deals more directly with issues of justice and the 'Make Poverty History' campaign, but there is also a lighter side to the darkness still ahead of us. A friend's comments on the earlier poems was: "Bill's poems are rubbish!" I offer that criticism as an alternative to the generous comments John Miller has made. You will judge for yourself, of course, but I hope these new poems will promote some discussion and may encourage further support for the work of Christian Aid. It is *not* yet too late. For the Christian, the light still shines in the darkness.

Acknowledgements

My thanks are due to friends and family who have read some or all of these verses and given helpful advice: Ian Balfour-Paul, Alistair Davidson, Mary Heyes, Paul Maxwell, James Rainy Brown, Dr. Robin Stewart and the late Very Rev. Dr. Bill Johnston.

My special thanks to the patient Sarah whose support and encouragement know no bounds and to James and Julia who have come to terms with their father's eccentricities.

John Lowrie Morrison welcomed Sarah and me to his delightful studio at Tayvallich and when he heard the book was to be published for Christian Aid he waived all fees and donated the two inspiring Jolomo transparences which will lighten the darkness for many readers.

I wrote to John Miller expecting the answer 'no' when I asked him to write a foreword to the book. Nothing has pleased me more than his generous response and support for this project.

My thanks also to the Rev. Dr. George Whyte, who has not only given active support to the *Make Poverty History* campaign, but approved a launch of the book in Colinton Parish Church where I serve as an elder.

Finally, I thank David McLeod of Makar Publishing whose invaluable support and advice made this production possible.

Justice
and
Peace

Anonymous

For a start
write these two names on your heart:
Ken Bigley and Margaret Hassan . . .
From today there can be no limit
to man's inhumanity to man.

Even if the video is too explicit
for us to see
the full extent of evil
the world must surely know
that this is the work of the devil.

When will it end . . . ?

Tonight,
I cannot sleep for fear
that somewhere in Iraq,
perhaps in the attack on Fallujah,
we may have killed some man or woman
who is as innocent
as Ken Bigley or Margaret Hassan.
Evil goes round in circles
and starts again.

Arms Sales

'I used to complain about my shoes
till I met a man who had no feet.'
I resolved there and then
never to complain about my shoes again.

Nothing can restore that man's feet.
All we can do is expose the obscenity
of those who benefit from the sale of arms
without a thought for victims who suffer
at the sharp end of it.

The simple choice is this:
either we shut our eyes to such injustices
or else we outlaw evil practices
which leave so many legless or maimed for life.

Beslan

God created man in his own image
with freedom to choose at any stage
between good and evil – a fine line
dividing the bestial from the divine.

But at Beslan we saw Satan in the flesh,
the light of day reduced to darkness
and the end of innocence.

Can you imagine your son or daughter
imprisoned in a gym without food or water
lying naked on the floor in fear?

The time has come for Islam to repent.
Surely every Imam is meant
to condemn the slaughter of the innocent
as they're taught in the Koran.

A bombshell

I'm sure you remember the story
of the woman caught in adultery.
The penalty then was death by stoning.
Christ had a different angle on this:
he called on the stoning party to confess.
"This poor woman," he said, "is not alone.
Let an innocent man cast the first stone."

Each of Christ's stories has a message of its own
which still speaks to us in this new century.
You can apply Christ's teaching to the present day
by substituting the word 'bomb' for 'stone'.

"Let those who are innocent drop the first bomb."

Crusading

Words can kill.
Take two examples –
JIHAD and INFIDEL.
Each in its own way
sends shock waves
through humanity.

There *is* another man-made word
which will divide and kill –
the word CRUSADE.
How could George Bush
have made such a basic error
as to call for a crusade,
a war on terror?

For pity's sake!
May he be forgiven
for such stupidity.
God only knows what terror is.
Even presidents may need to pray
for God's forgiveness.

Judgement

Once let your conscience go a-wandering
and soon the time will come
when right and wrong don't mean a thing.
You'll find it easier to fashion your morals
as you go along –
what's called moral relativity.

Tolerance becomes the in-thing.
Before long you'll find that
sin has lost its sting.
Once open that door
and you will tolerate anything,
except, of course, intolerance.

But, hold on!
Between you and me and our Creator,
we can be absolutely certain
that judgement will follow,
sooner or later.

A new rallying call

The five permanent members of the Security Council of the United Nations are responsible for 80% of the world's arms sales.

'There is a green hill far away
without a city wall',
but on Flanders Fields that winter's day
there was no green at all.
Men drowned there in a sea of mud.
The green grass was stained red with blood . . .
There was no life at all.

Humankind was never meant
to kill the young and innocent
before they'd lived at all, at all . . .
Before they'd lived at all.

Time now for us to shed fresh tears,
the bugle echoes down the years
with a new rallying call, a call,
a new rallying call.

It's surely unforgivable
that those who died so we might live
should find we haven't heard their call.
We haven't heard at all . . .

                              at all . . .

                                        at all . . .

The prize

How would you feel
if the Americans dubbed you
'the Axis of Evil'?

Neo-Conservatives seem miles away
from the world's reality
with their American dream.
Their certainty frightens me.

The prize they offer to Iraq
as compensation for the slaughter
of the innocent
is freedom and democracy.

Instead, the people of Iraq
may use the vote to seize their oil,
drive out the USA
and spread the Jihad.

Is that not politically astute
– what democracy's all about?

Race?

DNA suggests that homo sapiens
originates from one place.
We have more in common with our neighbours
than just a pretty face.
Do you know, for instance, that a single gene
determines the colour of our skin?
Those who claim to belong to a superior race
have got it wrong.
There is no such thing!

You remember apartheid,
a mixture of bad theology and science,
which led to gross discrimination
and exploited half the human race.

At that time
mixed marriages were frowned upon.
Now at last those racial barriers are down
and we are free to marry anyone,
black, white or brown.

Perhaps the time has come
to look again at St Peter's dream –
the vision where the unclean was declared clean.
Surely the one true God loves all his children ,
no matter what the colour of our skin.

1789

Liberty, equality, fraternity
were supposed to set the people free:
but that is not the lesson of history.

On the one hand,
Liberty leads to inequality.
In a free society
talent rises to the top
like a champagne cork which pops out of the bottle.
Before you know where you are
society is divided . . .
rich and poor.

On the other hand,
equality is Marxism or the communist way.
All people are not naturally equal,
you must compel them to be so
or else all corks will pop out of their bottles.
You must enforce equality,
which, as we all should know by now,
leads to inefficiency.

The only answer is fraternity,
which, as it happens, is God's way.
Those to whom God has given much must
share it with the rest of us
for the benefit of all humanity.

The Question

Well, wouldn't you have done the same . . . ?
The War, I mean. That monster Saddam Hussein,
with his mythical bunkers hiding WMD.
Death and Destruction less than an hour away from Israel
          and our essential Gulf oil . . .
Only the lilly-livered would reject the call
to war and like the anti-war brigade
do nothing at all.

My answer's 'No!'
Call me lilly-livered if you will,
but I still believe that war
is a self-fulfilling prophecy.
It is no way to set the world to rights.
Once 'let slip the dogs of war',
and before you know where you are
no man can rein them in again.

The wars in Afghanistan and Iraq
may not have caused the terrorist attack on London,
but they have undone much of the good work done
to bring together those of every race and religion
in this cosmopolitan city.
Now evil men have set alight a forest fire of violence
          and inflamed Jihadists who have no sense
                    of the *Brotherhood of Man*.
The time has come for every Imam to tell
these suicide bombers they will end in hell.

When?

I woke up this morning and thought of Darfur.
A scar on humanity . . .
one step too far.

Surely not again!

It was then I remembered
those days in Rwanda,
when our brothers and sisters
– Hutus and Tutsies –
destroyed one another,
spilling rivers of blood,
while we watched from afar
and did nothing about it.

Surely never again,
was what we said then.

When will we learn?
　　　When?
　　　　　When?
　　　　　　　When?

Make
Poverty
History

Geldof

The citizens of Edinburgh
went off Bob Geldof
before he went on stage.
When he invited a million
to our city without our ken,
that was more than enough.

But Geldof is a man of action
who gets things done,
and he has the good sense
to condemn all violence.

He knows that the way
to defeat the terrorist
is to end injustice.

Listen, if you dare,
to what he is saying to us:
"Thirty thousand children each day
          are dying
from *preventable* poverty."

Corruption?

Making Poverty History
is a matter of justice not charity.
Bankers who dismiss the whole idea
of debt cancellation and fair trade
should be made to read the economist,
Jeffrey Sachs,
or the no-nonsense Noreena Hertz.
They both know what justice is.

Do you imagine that banks
lent money to corrupt dictators
        out of charity?
Dismiss such ideas from your head
and instead look at the reality.
They lent surplus oil money
with an absolute guarantee
that no country could go bankrupt.
Even corrupt dictators' debts
would be repaid . . . sooner or later.

In this way,
it is the poorest on earth
who always have to pay.

Enough

'If you wish to make a man happy, add not to his possessions, but take away from his desires . . . To whom little is not enough, nothing is enough.' Epicurus

If people speak to you of riches,
and suggest that happiness lies
in the wealth you possess,
call their bluff.
No one is truly happy
who is not satisfied
with enough.

In this world I've found
there's enough,
but not more than enough
to go round.

Evangelical

Amongst the President's guests
was the evangelist, Jim Wallis,
invited to a faith based teach-in
held in the White House Roosevelt Room.

Many of his friends are evangelical,
so the President and Jim Wallis got on well,
but Wallis does not mince his words
and in no time they had crossed swords
(if you'll forgive the metaphor . . .).

Jim Wallis made his case:
"The real war against the terrorist
must be fought in the swamps of injustice.
The evils of terrorism will not fade away
until we wage war against the real enemy –
desperation and poverty . . ."

That was the moment when
George Bush gave his quizzical look,
and turned his back on Jim Wallis.
So far as 1 know
they have not spoken since.

I sometimes find it hard to tell
what George Bush means by evangelical.

Gordon Brown

'Therefore I have set my face like a flint.'
Isaiah 50.vs 7b RSV

Our Chancellor, Gordon Brown,
looks at life square on.
We all recognise the iron chin
but does anyone know for certain
what goes on within?

It is not too hard to guess
that Gordon is a son of the manse.
His old mother sent him a letter,
saying he should do better
with the cancelling of the debt.
"Don't send me a reply," she wrote,
"just put the stamp and this ten pound note
in the debt cancellation pot!"

Face to face

Perhaps in the distance,
well beyond the present reality,
life will at last make sense.

But why have we received your gift of grace,
when all around us here
we see people face to face
with poverty and despair?

Dear Lord, why do you allow
such inequality in the here and now?

In my saner moments I know
that we are here to do what we can
in the place where we are now.
The answer lies on some distant horizon
where we will see you face to face.

Greed

Sometimes I wonder
if we have one gene in common . . .
                greed.
The more we have
the more we seem to need.
In no time the earth falls victim
to conspicuous consumption.

Like a compost heap,
greed enriches the soil
on which terrorists feed.

Seeds of injustice
lead to green shoots of hate.
Not long to wait for the outcome;
suicide bombs, martyrdom and so on.

If we are serious in our prayer,
        'Thy Kingdom come,'
we must put our house in order
and share scarce resources
– land and clean water.
How else can our brothers and sisters
know what true justice is?

The hairs of our head

Christ tells us
that God notes the sparrow's fall,
and he also said
that he numbers all the hairs of our head.
Life is a game, a mystery
of what we do and do not know.
Even a few years ago,
no one would have known
that the DNA of mice and men
is much the same.

If the living God has made each one of us
(and the hyena and the hippopotamus),
he may choose to note the sparrow's fall;
and if he numbers all the hairs of our head,
that is surely much more than a holy metaphor.
It may be one sign in this game of life
that God loves us all the same,
numbers every hair of our head
and knows us each by name.

Heaven

Sometimes I fear
that I have had my heaven
here and now,
with any amount to eat and drink;
but I often lie awake and think
of Lazarus at the gate . . .

. . . and the millions who fade away
on less than a dollar a day.
Why should the rest of us
grow fat on earth's surpluses?
Let me tell you this, for what it is worth:
conspicuous consumption will one day end
this heaven on earth.

Hypocrisy

Don't blame the Germans alone.
The whole human race shares the blame for the holocaust.
Why do we turn a deaf ear and a blind eye
to the latest sufferings of humanity?
We still hide behind the smokescreen of yesterday.

But what of today?
Forget Rwanda . . . lost in our collective memory.
And as for Africa: the Rift Valley is much too far away.
We can walk by on either side
without noticing the genocide.
Instead we listen to the Press,
who tell us that Africa is a cesspool of corruption
with face-card dictators and their Swiss bank accounts.

How can we be guilty of such hypocrisy?
Have we not shown them the way
by lending them freely at *compound interest*,
and then refusing to cancel unpayable debt
from which we continue to profit?

I tell you this:
if we do not listen to the cries
of the poorest people on earth,
the evils of this new holocaust
will come home to roost
with us.

3 a.m. again

Lord Jesus,
I am lost in the mystery
of this world's wilderness.
Why don't you speak to us
again?

My son,
you ask the wrong question:
I am still speaking.
Why don't you listen to me
and do what I say:
'Make poverty history'.

Trade Justice

The World is divided –
the 'haves' and 'have nots'.
The 'haves' have much more than the 'have nots' have got,
and don't seem to care what the 'have nots' have not.
We stockpile the oil and build mountains of seed
and sell arms to poor countries – the last thing they need!
When they're desperate for medicines and wells for clean water,
we sell them small arms which just adds to the slaughter.

Oh! I nearly forgot
to tell what else happens to those who have not.
As you probably know the WTO
adjusts all the trade rules to go with the flow,
so the number of absolute poor is growing
and the rich become richer without even knowing.

As one of the 'haves', I don't understand
why we banish the 'have nots' to cloud cuckoo land.
Remember that Jubilee Day at Cologne
when we heard the good news! If only we'd known
that the promises made to cancel the debt
would still be on the back-burner as yet.
The 'haves' have such power that often it seems
our hopes are no more than ephemeral dreams.

The wall

Beware of the Neo-Conservatives,
enclosed within their wall of certainty
that has no foundation at all
outside the USA.

Why do they close their eyes
to the sufferings of distant humanity?
Surely it must be hypocrisy
to preach the good news
only to those who choose
to vote for you.

Why cast into outer darkness
those who live in a distant continent?
Whatever Neo-Conservatives may claim,
that is not what Christ meant.

A
Time
to
Smile

Bladon races

Sarah was eight months pregnant at the time,
when a police car flagged her down
for driving too fast through Bladon.

The policeman peered in and was going to say,
"Madam, you're driving much too fast."
When he saw she was in the family way,
he changed his mind and smiled at last.
"Madam," he said, "this won't do at all.
You'd better speed on to the hospital!"

Golf: the Bishop of London

The Bishop went north on the night express
to rest from his labours at Inverness.
He stopped in St Andrews, as wise men do,
to play golf on the Old Course – a round or two.

Lord Bishops don't play with just any body.
He was paired with the famous Andra Kirkaldy,
renowned for his game throughout the land,
who knew the Old Course like the back of his hand.

The Bishop was quite an ordinary player
but he usually escaped from the bunkers by prayer.
For thirteen holes he played out of his skin
but his shot to Hell's Bunker went fatally in.

"Tak yer niblick, Lord Bishop, ye'll no get oot."
But the Bishop had ither plans nae doot.
A lightning prayer and he called for his spoon,
then he blasted his ball half way to the moon.

To get oot o' Hell's Bunker you need yer niblick.
Such divine intervention made Andra feel sick.
"Let me tell you, Lord Bishop, when ye come tae dee,
mak sure that ye tak yer auld spoon wi ye!"

Chocolate Biscuits

The Mother Superior of the girls'school
believed in good manners and discipline.
At St Teresa's they all stick to the rule,
in assemblies no girl would dare drop a pin.

At night all girls go to the Refectory
for prayer and a bite of light refreshment.
There is always a hot drink and apples for supper . . .
low on calories but high on nourishment.

The Mother Superior had written a warning note
beside the bowl of apples in full view.
'Take one apple only girls,' she wrote.
'You can be certain that God is watching you!'

Chocolate biscuits were also on the table
with a rough note written by one of the girls.
'Eat as many biscuits as you are able.
God has his eye on the apples!'

Jazz

The angel Gabriel sings Mozart in his bath,
> but Bach on Holy Days.
On other days, or so they say,
> all the angels sing along on plainsong.

> But God is said to have a soft spot
for improvisation – JAZZ – that just goes on and on
> > with no set score or text.
> He delights to see what these mortals
> > he loves so much and has set free
> > > will get up to next.

London Town

Desmond Tutu always looks on the bright side.
It would have taken more than apartheid
to undermine his love of life and laughter.

In student days at King's College he would have some fun
and occasionally do those things he ought not to have done.
Although Tutu knew every nook and cranny, every street,
when he spotted a London bobby on the beat
he would cross the road to hear the policeman say:
"Can I help you, Sir, you seem to have lost your way?"

By this simple act of racial courtesy,
the London bobby may have shown the way
from the dark days of apartheid to the Rainbow Nation,
and the miracle of Truth and Reconciliation.

Sir Malcolm Rifkind

Our old friend Malcolm Rifkind
has gone south to pastures new.
Member for Chelsea now, we hear
– sounds like a flower show.

The English may see themselves as the chosen race;
but it takes a Scot to put them in their place.
Sir Malcolm is particularly good at that,
having all the skills of the natural diplomat.

When a London journalist asked him why
Kensington and Chelsea had chosen yet another Scot,
Sir Malcom with the usual twinkle in his eye
replied that, "None of us is perfect."

Misalliance

John was sitting in the stalls and he was eagerly awaiting
the start of Madam Butterfly. His keen anticipating
was rudely interrupted when a lady was delayed
and entered to his row just as the overture was played.

They all stood up to let her make her way along the row,
each person standing up and down just like a domino.
John rose reluctant to his feet and happened to look down
where he saw to his embarrassment his trouser zip undone.

As an elegant young lady in a ballgown drifted past,
he seized the opportunity to do up his zip at last.
Imagine his confusion when he looked down to find
that her ballgown and his zip were inextricably entwined.

There was no way this alliance could be easily undone,
so they both went back along the row pretending they were one.
They found a pair of scissors to cut themselves apart,
but the moment they were parted it nearly broke John's heart.

When the opera was over they had supper and champagne
and enjoyed each other's company so they planned to meet again.
They were married the next year and lived happily ever after
and every time John told this tale their house was filled with
      laughter.

Pocket money

The old adage
that 'the Child is Father of the Man'
applied to James aged nine.
Early one morning without any warning
he said, to my surprise,
"Dad, any chance of a rise?
My pocket money's 80 per cent below
the national average!"

Pillion ride

Pat McSwinney, a master at Merchiston,
who had just arrived home from his honeymoon,
decided to take his charming young wife
on a theatre trip she'd remember for life.

His new motor bike (five hundred ccs)
would get to The King's in ten minutes with ease.
With his wife on the pillion and holding on tight,
they set off for town in the cool of the night.

Like young Lochinvar who was proud of his steed,
Pat rode as the wind. . .with breakneck speed.
He arrived at The King's, but to his despair
when he looked round, his young wife was not there.

When the lights turned green at Craiglockhart she'd found
that she was left stranded both feet on the ground.
The moral is clear . . . whatever the weather,
if you're out with your wife, you should stick close together.

No smoke without fire

My wife was down in town that day and to her great surprise
she saw a schoolboy smoking – she could not believe her eyes.
That morning in assembly I had spoken to the school
and warned them yet again about the 'No Smoking' rule.

My wife was very careful when it came to discipline.
Unless the offence was serious, she would never run boys in.
On many an occasion, she would turn a blind eye;
but this smoking was so blatant she could hardly just walk by.

I summoned the offender and said that I had heard
he'd been smoking down in town. Ian said, "This is absurd.
As I'm sure you are aware, Sir, I would never let you down.
Nothing would persuade me to light up down in town."

He wondered if I'd made a simple error in identity.
"There are many boys who smoke," he said. "I could easily
        name you twenty.
May I ask you, Sir, to tell me how you knew that it was me."
(His grammar was uncertain as I'm sure that you will see.)

"The person who reported you described the boy so well
that I knew it must be you . . . it wasn't hard to tell.
She said the boy was handsome, dark and very tall."
"You're absolutely right, Sir. It was me after all!"

The Old Firm

Glasgow's no place for Sassenachs and strangers
on Old Firm days when Celtic's playing Rangers.
A neutral spectator in the North Stand found
the fans were making such a sound
with their obscenities that he wondered what to do!
Their behaviour was an insult to the game he loved and knew.

He stood in solemn silence and the truth, I fear,
is that when a goal was scored, he didn't even cheer.
He was lost in admiration when Celtic showed their skill,
yet when Rangers scored another goal he stood in silence still.

The crowd on either side of him could not believe their ears:
a solemn Celtic/Rangers fan who never even cheers.
"Kick him oot the ground," they cried, "he'll no be missed.
We're a' true believers here, but he's an atheist!"

71

By the time you're seventy–one
your life is running down,
which is not much fun for anyone.
The best thing to do
is to run the straight race,
one day at a time,
at one hell of a pace.

Tantrums

Our children listen
to what we say,
and try out our language
in their very own way.

One morning at Nursery
a furious two-year-old
was having a tantrum,
as two–year–olds do.

Peter aged two
who's his father's son
came out with a phrase
he had heard at home . . .

"Keep your hair on!"

A time to smile

I asked this Kenyan girl
why Africans always seem to smile.
She laughed.
"Where we live," said Malinde,
"the sun shines every day.
We just sit in the sun
and talk the day through,
from sunrise to sundown!"

"Yes, that's all very well,
but tell me about all the poverty.
It's quite hard to smile on a dollar a day."

Malinde replied:
"As you know, we've not much to spare,
so we all get together and share.
If you share all you have,
and no one's left out,
then you all have something to smile about!"

Up in the morning early

We have all been there before.
A child's high chair
is not a debating chamber.

Not yet two,
Peter knew quite well
what he wanted to do . . .
So he blew two raspberries at breakfast,
noises which stopped the flow.

"Stop that, Peter," says Mum,
"or you go upstairs."
So then he blew an outrageous raspberry,
just to see what Mum would do.

At the time it seemed hard
but out came the yellow card,
and Peter was off to his cot . . .
Like it or not, even at two,
children must learn
what they may not do.

A
Time
to
Think

Aims

No doubt about it.
If you aim at nothing,
you generally hit it.
Young people are not to blame
if we don't give them something to aim at.

The key to education is encouragement.
Children have a deep-set fear of defeat,
but concealed within them is some hidden fire
– secret aims to which they aspire,
but are afraid to share with us.

The aim of teaching
is to unlock Pandora's box,
release their fears and uncertainties,
and lead them on their journeys
to new horizons.

The Butterfly

You all know the story of the philosopher
who dreamt he was a butterfly.
He woke from the dream
to the reality – or so it seemed –
of the sunshine in a bright blue sky.

Confusion. How was he now to know
what to believe?
Was he a philosopher
who had been dreaming in bed
or was he a lovely butterfly instead?

As we all know today,
there is little difference anyway
between a philosopher and a butterfly . . .
They have much the same DNA!

Creation

When I first saw her tiny finger nails
I had no further need to wonder.
They bore the imprint of God's miracle
and told creation's tale.

Every creature is part of God's creation,
bound down and ordered
by the laws of gravity
and other laws besides.

But man alone
is part of the greater story
told to the glory of God.

We alone are subject to the moral order
of the word, written into history
by the Creator.

God has given to each of us
our own obstacle course to run,
with freedom to choose our own way,
right or wrong.

Choose carefully.
Choice matters at the end of the day.

Enemies

If God is for us,
does it matter who's against us?
Well, yes, it does.

Christ told us to love our enemies.
Somehow we must master the hatred
that is a recipe for disaster
when it masters us.

The only way
to know why our enemies hate us
is to love them as our neigbour,
and listen to what they say.

Free-falling

If at first you don't succeed,
bungee-jumping's not for you.
Human life takes understanding:
no point in launching into space
unless you have a place for landing.

A blissful life of endless spending
leads to the debtor's fall from grace.
False dreams of happiness extending
land up in a rocky place
with debts beyond the elastic's ending.

Always save for the rainy day.
In Scotland it's not far away.

Enlightenment

What was it that once made Scotland great?
Was it the tradition to educate all our children
or was it the fact that the Scots are a race apart,
born in a rocky place with an independence of heart?

Something must explain the globe-trotting Scot.
Travel the world and you'll find, as like as not,
a Scotsman in every port of call
and a Scottish doctor in the hospital.
Worldwide trade unions are often led
by a glottal-stopping Scot, aggressively articulate,
immovable as the Bass Rock or the rock of Ailsa Craig.

But wait, still no answer to my question:
'What was it that made Scotland great?'
Was it the Celtic vision of a transcendent God
or their education system which was somewhat odd
with Minister and Dominie leading the way
through classless access to the university?

Or did it all start with the Reformation,
John Knox, six feet above perdition, in full flow
holding forth in St Giles for three hours at one go?
Or was it all the other goings-on of religion . . .
– Bishops and Covenanters and so on –
later culminating in the Great Disruption?

****

What made Scotland great is now history.
It matters little or not at all
in comparison with the mystery of our decline and fall.
What part did the Enlightenment play
in the rise and fall of Scotland's history?

We all know about Scottish philosophy . . .
Dugald Stewart, David Hume and such as they,
laid the foundation of the first globalization
that gave the Scots their world-wide reputation.

But it was Adam Smith who opened the gateway
to prosperity – mass production and the liberalisation of trade.
From his time on the Scots have been amongst the best
at creating wealth and feathering their own nest.

But by a curious paradox it was also the Enlightenment
that led the way to our decline and fall.
It is true that Scotland led the way
to the nineteenth century imperial prosperity:
soldiers, explorers and engineers all made their mark
and missionaries brought light to many a dark
corner of the globe. Profit, of course, was not forgotten.
Our looms clothed naked natives with our cotton.

But material success and secularization
were to prove the downfall of the Scottish nation.
Instead of worshipping the one true God transcendent
man worshipped the finite and dependent
mind of man and left God out of the equation.
We took the fast lane to wealth creation
to satisfy ourselves and, as we know so well,
'The love of money is the root of all evil.'
There really is no point at all
in gaining the whole world
and losing our own soul.

Labels

Most of us
who try to follow Christ
label each other
either 'liberal' or 'evangelical'.

Labels (and League Tables)
identify us and divide.
So shall we decide,
as far as we are able,
not to use a label?

Those who are serious
about sowing gospel seed
find that 'Christian'
is the only label we need.

Mixed blessings

Cultural arrogance is a loathsome disease.
Please, whatever you do,
never impose your culture
on those who see life differently.

We are all on the same journey
to a far country;
but we start from where we are
and learn from each other
along the way.

Never, whatever you do
and however sure you may be,
close your neighbour's door
to eternity.

Message to the USA

You too will have heard
of Desmond Tutu.
When asked by the BBC
what the USA should do,
he said:
"They should share prosperity,
       trade fairly
              and end poverty!"

Over to you.

Scots Wha Hae

As a nation
we Scots are renowned
for self-deprecation.
John Calvin still makes his mark
and has left us imprisoned by the dark
without and the sin within.
Guilt-ridden by what we have done
        (or left undone)
we seldom seem to win.

'We'll pay for it, we'll pay for it, we'll pay for it,'
as the poet has so wisely written.*

There is more to the Scot than meets the eye.
You just can't keep a good Scot down.
Smitten by self-deprecation we may be;
but if you allow me one word of prophecy
        it is this . . .
Scotland will rise again in this century.

*Scotland, *Weathering*, Alastair Reid (1978)

Water

'Praised be my Lord for our Sister Water, who is very serviceable unto us and humble and precious and clean.' St Francis of Assisi

Wisdom, as you know,
flows down to us like water from the past
as part of our inheritance.

Do you know that every bottle
of water contains at least one molecule
of H_2O that was drunk by Aristotle?
So every time we take a glass of water
we should think of past wisdom,
link the past to the present
and drink to the future.

A
Time
to
Listen

Guantanamo Bay

O wad some Pow'r the giftie gie us
To see oursels as others see us . . .

To A Louse, Robert Burns

In the morning when I'm praying
I think carefully what I'm saying.
At the crack of dawn each day
God may listen to what I say.

But when I prayed this morning
God gave two clear words of warning
and insisted that I listen
to what he had to say . . .
        Guantanamo Bay.

What did you say, Lord . . .
Guantanamo Bay?
Frankly it has nothing to do with me,
nothing at all.
I leave all that to Amnesty International.

What – use our imagination . . .
get inside the skin of Osama bin Laden . . .
see ourselves as bin Laden sees us!

You just can't be serious, Lord.
Why should we see ourselves
through sinners' eyes?

So what do you mean, Lord?
Surely the Coalition
rescued Afghanistan from the Taliban
and then struck again
to topple the monster, Saddam Hussein.

Is there some great dividing line
between the way we see ourselves
and the way bin Laden sees us?

Where we may see the American dream,
he sees an Islamic nightmare
a world of corruption and despair . . .
Where we may see a just war,
he sees an abuse of power.
Where we may bring liberation,
he feels humiliation
and a threat to Islam.

I'm just beginning to hear what you say, Lord.
Perhaps we should think again about Camp X-Ray.
Even one of the thieves at Golgotha
was given a fair hearing
denied to all those
at Guantanamo Bay.

The Present

We are prisoners in time and space.
Often it seems that we cannot escape
from the place and time where we are.
The media add fuel to the flames
and set fire to our hopes and certainties.
Life passes by one day at a time,
seen as a series of snapshots
caught in the eye of the storm.

There is more to this life
than the snapshots of each single day.
Take time out to listen . . .
The wind still blows in from the sea
and surely you hear distant waves
as they break on the shore
of our destiny.

A Time to Listen

Sometimes, I don't know anyone
unless I sit down and listen to them.
All of us have our stories to tell,
but we seldom know each other well enough
to sit down and listen to our stories.

Today, I walked past a hundred folk
on Princes Street and I have no doubt
they all had their stories to tell.
Often you have to go to a funeral
to hear the Minister tell the story in full.
(Our Minister does this particularly well.)
But surely we should strive
to share our stories
while we're still alive.

How about today?
Have we time to sit down
and hear what each of us has to say?

The Secret Garden

When night falls
after a busy day,
I retreat into the secret garden
                     of the heart.
High time to batten down the hatches
and think what life is all about.

Is life all about present love and laughter
        – the here and now –
with no thought about the hereafter?
Or is life's journey teleological
        with some clear end in view after all?

Start from the secret garden of the heart.
Deep in the tangled shrubbery of the mind
        there in the walled garden you will find
the Lord Christ to guide you through
        to another day.

No one else seems to know the way.

Spin

Alastair Campbell,
New Labour spin doctor,
welcomed this heckler
like a hole in the head.
When he asked his odd question
which referred to 'our Maker',
Campbell replied,
         "We do not do God!"

God, in his wisdom,
may not give a jot
whether Alastair Campbell
does him or not.

But if Labour's spin doctor
would raise his sights higher,
and just use his eyes,
he might well be surprised
at what God does for *us*.

London

MACDUFF: *Such welcome and unwelcome things at once*
    'Tis hard to reconcile.
        Macbeth: Act 4. Scene 3

On the day before,
their dream came true.
London shared euphoria
with Lord Coe and his Olympic team
in Singapore.
This was the London we knew,
  open to the sky,
    with a welcome for every passer-by
      regardless of race or religion.

But on the morning after,
disaster struck.
The bombers blew apart . . .
or so they thought . . .
the very heart of London.
More than fifty died,
  innocently going about their business
    like the rest of us.

Little did the bombers know
  that nothing breaks the heart of London,
nor can bombs undo what London has done
    and will do again.

Thank God that so many Muslims
now stand shoulder to shoulder
with their friends and fellow citizens.
There can be no place for violence
in a city where we learn together
that freedom and the rule of law
  are the essence.

Buds
of
Heaven

Anno Domini (in a nutshell)

In the beginning God said,
"Let there be light,"
and there was light: day and night,
      and he saw that it was good.

That was just the start.
The wonder of his creative art,
with all the endless beauty
of earth and sky and sea,
would make no sense at all
without a human audience.

Adam and Eve, if you like,
      were the risk God took.
From the Garden of Eden on, God could tell
that man would use his freedom to rebel.
Even today we can see the truth of Genesis,
      the Adam and Eve and apple myth,
            however unfashionable that truth may be.
At the heart of the matter lies our greed:
      we love to devour the seed corn with the seed.

Strange as it may seem,
      the dream became reality
         when God created time and space,
      with man his masterpiece in his own image.
His plan was that the whole human race
would be free to worship him.

He revealed his law through his prophets,
but even his chosen race was slow to listen.
Such was the chaos and confusion
that at one appointed time in history,
      the incarnation,
         God sent his son.

This was the moment when the myth became reality,
when God in the flesh entered time and space
and shared the suffering of the human race.
Life made sense at last
through this mystery of salvation.
God gave to us the living bread
in Jesus Christ his Son.

Be still

Psalm 46: verse 10

Be still and know that I am God.
Be still and know.
Be still . . .

How can we hear the still small voice
and know God's will,
if we surround ourselves
with a cacophony of sound?
Instead, try silently listening
in the stillness of the night.

Beauty

No one can explain beauty.
It is a matter of soul, not eye,
and lightens the darkness within
as a rainbow brightens the sky.

Now as the years go by,
a rose is no more than a rose to me.
But sometimes I see in your soul
what to me is a rose in its beauty.

Christmas – or God with us

It does seem odd, even absurd,
to choose one theological word
        – *incarnation* –
to welcome the Son of God.

No wonder so many seem clueless
        about the real Jesus.
Theologians confuse us
        with words which seem meaningless.
Women (and even men maybe!)
        prefer to cuddle a baby
                than to study theology.

Would it not be wiser
for us to close our eyes,
        and imagine the real Jesus,
                no longer a baby,
but God present with us
        in our suffering and uncertainty?

A gift

Yesterday is history
Tomorrow is mystery
Today is a gift . . .

Eternity
      may be no more than a breath away.
There is nothing to fear . . .
Death is a mere question mark ,
      a candle of light in our darkness.

The whole book of life is seamless, unending.
All that once was and is still to be
is there to be seen . . . recorded indelibly.
The network of memory runs endlessly on
      to rise like the first light of day
         at the dawn of eternity.

Homecoming

Once upon a time,
John decided to leave home.
As you may have guessed,
he was an adolescent, ready to fly the nest
– Sydney, Rome – anywhere away from home . . .
Dad and Mum were driven to despair,
but they saw him off with his share
of the nest egg and a prayer.

The rest of the story you can guess.
Sex, drinking, drugs and so on –
all the dreadful things that go on
in a foreign land, Gap Year unplanned . . .

To cut the story short,
he made a pig's breakfast of it.
Sadly, I have to report
that the time soon came
when he hadn't a bean to his name.

In these dire circumstances
John came to his senses,
got on his mobile phone
and called Dad from Capetown.

Dad e-mailed a ticket
and when John landed at Gatwick
the following day there was his Dad,
waving a welcome home flag
on the runway.

God's rainbow

Blood, toil, tears and sweat . . .

Not I . . . . I look up.
There's more to life than mud,
sweat, tears, toil and blood.
Raise your eyes with me
and you may see
God's rainbow in the sky.

Inside out

Don't be afraid.
You're not the only one
living in a state of confusion.
We all lose our way now and again.

Why not try this recipe?
Before the day's begun,
rise with the sun
and read The Sermon on the Mount.
There Christ teaches us about
the world we live in
set in the context of the next.

Read on . . .
      the time will come when
           our inside out world
               will turn outside in again.

When seen in the light of eternity
even our present confusion
will make sense again.

The Mountain Top

Somehow we have to look beyond today
with its abuse and cruelty.
Switch off the TV, tear up the tabloids.
Spend three days away on some mountain top
        and pray.

The breath of the Spirit blows gently there.
Fresh air on the mountain top assures us
there is life before death.
Three days away and you will know for certain
that this life is not the only reality.
Heaven on earth is no more than a breath away.

Renewables

The burning Bush is fuelled by coal and oil;
but the desert bush which stayed alight
and burned continuously throughout the night
was fuelled by the power of God
which, odd as it may seem, is renewable
like all good fuels.

President Bush might learn more
if he listened to the teaching of John Muir,
as Teddy Roosevelt did.
God is to be found in unexpected places
and speaks to us from his wildernesses.

Resurrection

The best news of all
        is that Jesus Christ was seen alive again,
            the so-called Resurrection.

Not all the powers of hell
        could stop those witnesses
            from telling what they saw.

The news spread like wildfire
        after Pentecost.
Those who were lost found hope again.

Still, in the twenty-first century,
        the worldwide celebration goes on,
with universal communion
        in the shared bread and wine.

Candles

You can't rely on candles
to give you light.
When the wind blows,
candles go out.
The lack of candle light
no longer bugs me.
When I lie awake at night,
a candle burns internally.
I believe the Holy Spirit is the flame
lightening my darkness.

Pope John Paul the Second

Beware of the misanthrope
who looks on the dark side of life
as though there is no future hope.

Look instead
at the life of Pope John Paul.
Even when he couldn't speak at all,
he still shared the Easter message
of the life to come with everyone.
In death he lightened the darkness
that still lies ahead for us,
and was able to tell the whole world
that 'All shall be well'.

Cycling Singalongs

Jubilee Scotland

Tune: *Uist Tramping Song* by John R. Bannerman,
arranged by Hugh S. Roberton

Chorus
Come along, come along,
      let us cycle all together.
Come along, come along,
      be it fair or stormy weather.
With the Perthshire hills before us,
      let us all join in the chorus
and the G8 can't ignore us,
      when they hear this song.

Verse 1
We invite you all along,
      come and join us in our singing.
You don't *all* have to cycle,
      but please keep the music ringing.
It really is no mystery,
      turning poverty to history,
but the G8 have to listen
      to this song that we all sing.   *Chorus*

Verse 2
Now the first step we believe
      and it hasn't happened yet
is to hold them to their promises
      and CANCEL ALL THE DEBT.
If the G8 fail to listen
      on the 2nd of July
then even more poor children
      will inevitably die.   *Chorus*

Verse 3
The next thing that we need
      are FAIRER RULES OF TRADE.
In a global free trade system
      it's the poor who are betrayed.

The poorest people suffer
        when the rich world calls the tune,
so we'd better change the trade rules
        and we'd better change them soon.   *Chorus*

Verse 4
Turning poverty to history
        is the change that must be made
and the third aim of our campaign
        is MORE AND BETTER AID.
So let's sing one final chorus
        and we'll carry all before us,
but there won't be satisfaction
        till the G8 PROMISE ACTION.   *Chorus*

Cycling Along

Tune: *Westering Home* by Hugh S Roberton.

Chorus
Cycling along with a song in the air.
CANCEL THE DEBT now and end their despair.
Give them FAIR TRADE and the RIGHT KIND OF AID
and support our campaign in Scotland.

Verse 1
Join in our chorus and all sing along
The poor world has suffered for far far too long.
Make this the year we shall never forget.
End the world poverty – CANCEL THE DEBT.   *Chorus*

Verse 2
This is the year when we all should unite
to fight for TRADE JUSTICE and put the world right.
Why should the poorest on earth have to die?
Join our campaign at the start of July.   *Chorus*